GW00393291

Gallery Books
Editor Peter Fallon
THE SILENCE CAME CLOSE

Kerry Hardie

THE SILENCE CAME CLOSE

Gallery Books

The Silence Came Close
is first published
simultaneously in paperback
and in a clothbound edition
on 22 September 2006.

The Gallery Press
Loughcrew
Oldcastle
County Meath
Ireland

www.gallerypress.com

*All rights reserved. For permission
to reprint or broadcast these poems,
write to The Gallery Press.*

© Kerry Hardie 2006

ISBN 1 85235 408 9 *paperback*
      1 85235 409 7 *clothbound*

ISBN 978 1 85235 408 4 *paperback*
      978 1 85235 409 1 *clothbound*

A CIP catalogue record for this book
is available from the British Library.

Contents

for my cousin Rosaleen Jolley
and my friend Marian Tierney
with love and profound respect for their courage

Burrowing Creatures

Hawthornden Castle, Scotland

There's a poem I'm always trying to write. It always begins the same way. *Oh listen, listen —*

It is the urgency behind the words that compels me. I know what the poem is about, it's about the world and its shining. But what comes after these words is an emptying space.

Now I sit at the open window watching the sunlight lighting the mossy branches of the unleafed trees. I hear the cawing of nesting rooks, the rushing of waters deep in the glen. There are molehills pimpling the lawn below me, more of them every morning. They upset the Administrator; each day he is more distressed. The lawn slopes down from the woods and has long since been taken by moss; now the molehills erupt in purplish indiscipline across its face. Myriad molehills, destroying the order of lichen and grass. You can see that the owner is ageing, her sight failing, her hands losing their grip. Moles have exquisite hands. I have seen them, dead, and hooked to the barbed wire of fences. Their hands are like paddles, their fingers jointed and short.

The barbed wire fence is the modern form of a gibbet. Dead crows and foxes and moles are hung out in lines for the living to glance at their fate and stay clear. The scaffold, set at the crossroads or mounted high on the walls. I suppose it made sense. Seeing your neighbour swinging about in the wind might well stop you in your tracks. But how would it work for moles? Moles are all but blind and, anyway, live underground.

> Wait, it's coming again,
> *Oh listen, listen —*
> The shining rises up with the words,
> then dies down into the dark.

OF HARMONY

The Birch Tree

A small perfect tree,
its leaves green and gold,
standing alone
in the pasture.

I sit in the dew-soaked grass,
sit in the stillness,
watching its papered leaves
untie and fall.

Flesh

Sitting in a doorway,
in October sunlight,
eating
peppers, onions, tomatoes,
stale bread sodden with olive oil —

and the air high and clean,
and the red taste of tomatoes,
and the sharp bite of onions,
and the pepper's scarlet crunch —

the body
coming awake again,
thinking,
maybe there's more to life than sickness,
than the body's craving for oblivion,
than the hunger of the spirit to be gone —

and maybe the body belongs in the world,
maybe it knows a thing or two,
maybe it's even possible
it may once more remember

sweetness,
absence of pain.

Mushrooms and Cats

for Mary Loughlin

It is hot in October's hot sun up here in the mountains.
The sun streams through the doorway where I sit.
I think of going to walk about on the hillside.
I think of waiting till later when it cools.

Yesterday, climbing the track past the cows with the bells,
we found a great circle of mushrooms under the trees.
We laughed when we saw them there, couched in damp
    shadow,
then fell on them, calling out pleasure and greed.

The baskets were full, the evening was thickening,
we walked past the small dun cows with the pointed horns
and those eyes any woman with any sense would kill for —
the baskets were heavy all the way home.

Now the sun is skiting about in a sundance of dazzle
just over the rim of the mountain. Soon it will drop
and the gold trees will haze,
and the spider-lines threading the light will be dimmed.

Then I'll put on my boots and go and hunt mushrooms.
I want them for Mary — to find at her door —
when she moves from the fire to feed the night cats
that gather and crouch as the darkness sets fast.

Neighbours

We were sitting together, the four of us, eating, and there was a knock at the door. Cesca got up, she opened it and stood speaking, then took the woman there by the hand and drew her inside. She said, 'This is Anna'. We got up, went forward, she held us and kissed us, one kiss on each cheek the way they do here, even with strangers.

The woman said she'd heard that a Frenchman was staying. She had a letter she'd written in French but it wasn't right — not yet. She stood there, she shone with reluctance, eagerness, shyness; there were folded pages half hidden away in her hand. A sheepdog, she said, a dog that was trained and ready to sell, and a buyer had phoned her from France, from the other side of the Pyrenees. What could she do? His accent was strong, she'd forgotten her French, she had told him she'd write him a letter.

We looked at the man who should have been French. He said he was French-Canadian, said he would look at the letter, said if she wanted he'd go through it now with her, while she was here, it could be in the post the next day.

She didn't want to — a man with no eyes in his head could have seen that — she wanted to set the letter down on the table and run. But also she wanted to sell this dog, or she wouldn't have stayed. She was in her forties, hair fading, skin fading, fearful yet fearless, everything beautiful, like a late rose.

Cesca gave her some wine, and she sat by the French-Canadian, holding on tight to the letter, trying to smile a real smile. She gave him the pages. Talk started again and she made herself small behind it. He read with a pen in his hand and sometimes he asked her a question, then made a correction. We knew to go on with the talk and not watch.

It was like being at home in Ireland but everything happened in Catalan or French.

And the room was a cave stuffed with baskets and pictures and books, with cooking and music, the rafters were threaded with mushrooms and peppers and gourds, with rose-hips on strings. It was like being inside the pomegranate we'd just eaten. Packed tight with treasures, five-sided, six-sided, each seed set close and essential. And winter outside, moving huge in the night, and Persephone, deep down under the world, eating red jewels in the dark.

Again

Spring comes roundly,
as the round calls of pigeons
in the early morning.

March is starry with celandines.
Catkins hang
in falls of yellow rain.

In unleafed woods
the beer-brown pools stretch creaturely
as hares in the clean light.

Museum of Life in the Mountains

She showed us the place where the grain was stored,
its false front of glass,
the cheeses thrust deep in its dry warmth for winter storage.

She showed us the floor, its small stones set proud
so the snow from the sabots
ran off in the runnels between.

She showed us the upper room, not often used,
the plates from Granada displayed on the dresser,
the heavy carved armoire, its door left ajar
to hint at the plenty within.

Last of all, the *cremalls* — the heart of the house —
a black iron frame,
complex with arms, with mysterious hooks
that held the pots over the fire.

Fire and food —
the life of the flesh — the angel, descended —
strength in the hands, massed muscle in legs,
the sun in the grass,
in the bellies of goats,
of sheep and of cows,
the sun in the cheese
                    stored deep in the sun-ripened grain.

Flood

Each time I pass there are more swans.
A sedgy field at the best of times.
And the little hills, circling.
And the sag of the sky.

A slow file of cows
treads through a gap in the thorns
under a blaze of white light
that spills through a gap in the sky.

More swans, more water.
The coil of their necks
as they loop and they stretch,
as they puddle the rushy pasture.

Nine today — and the shine
of the low, cold light
on the stretch of the flood —
nine in the wet, mossed grass.

Each time I pass there is more water.
More water, more swans.
And cows, trudging up the green hill.
And the big-bellied sky, great with rain.

The Butcher's Wife

for Alex

She was thin
and bony and strong, with eyes
that had wept — you could see that — dark hair
that was greying — too busy for dye —
and patient and quick,
she minced lamb, sliced *serrano*,
sent off the son
to fetch the sheep's cheese — two different kinds —
explained their relative
hardness and softness; her mother
came in from the hall
bearing loops of raw sausage
like bicycle tyres,
went back to the back —
her slippered slap
on the red passage-tiles
before the door closed —
and the butcher's wife
was cutting the cheese,
her apron, washed soft,
had lace at the top and sides of the bib,
it had blood on the linen, blood on the lace,
and Lorca had stuck his head round the door,
still looking for signs
that are ancient and bare,
like blood,
like white linen,
like the loop of her hair, working loose.

Near Loughrea

The lone bull
red on an emerald ground.
The ruined church
through the gap-toothed wall.

Fields
bright with new grass, new lambs.
Sky
gone suddenly spacious and blue.

And the whitethorn breaking.
And the blackthorn making stars.

And one chestnut, standing holy,
its birth-wet buds
held to the high, wide sky.

OF STRIFE AND CONFLICT

Winter Mountains

for Melanie Rabat

Each day it grows colder.
The mountains edge closer.
Their maws open wider
to swallow the sun.

Each day they grow fiercer,
they eat the sun sooner.
It gnaws at their entrails,
ferments in their bellies.
They plunge like night horses,
they rear up, then spew out

the beaten
gold horn of the moon.

Visiting Eastern Europe

She took the jug from the table and the soap from the dish and the basin from the floor and we went outside. She set the basin down on the steps and quarter-filled it. She dipped her hands into the water and started to work them around the soap.

Thorough. Taking her time.

Her hands were broad and short and strong, the skin was tanned from the summer that had almost passed, the nails cut short and straight across. Not fancy hands but not rough either.

She knelt on the step and I stood over her with the pitcher. When she'd finished her soaping and cleaning she gestured for me to pour water. I tilted the jug; a small steady stream spilled from its lip. She moved her hands under this narrow flow till the soap was all washed away. She soaped them again, then she signalled a second time. I poured. She looked up at me and smiled and I smiled back. She took the towel from the rail and she dried her hands. Her hair had chestnut lights in the sun and behind her the flowers that are called a name that means 'the Innkeeper's Wife' stood bright and simple and strong.

I had never helped an adult wash her hands before. Hair, yes, but not hands. I liked it, liked the way we were together, the way it used less water and her hands were cleaner. Then there was the attentiveness, and the need to wait courteously. Her acceptance that made me quiet and calm.

She gestured to ask would I like her to do it for me? I shook my head. I liked it all, but I hadn't yet reached that place, could not yet bow. It didn't matter, the stretching shadows joined things up, the place moved nearer with each hour that passed.

I went down the steps and sat on the sparse, dry grass in the scrawny splotched shade of a plum tree. She carried the basin to where the tomatoes were wilting, selected a plant, poured out the water to seep to its roots.

Later, the heat began to slide back and a wind sprang up, stirring the leaves in the light that was golden and thick now as honey.

A woman came down the path and stopped by the rusty gate and pushed it open. Her skin was tanned and her body was easy and she was still beautiful. She raised her hands to her head, pulled them through her white hair and spoke to us in broken English. She didn't like the wind, she said, there was headache in it, and sickness — Had we heard of Chernobyl?

The man of the house came out of the house and the white-haired woman sat at the table and drank a glass of the milk that a kerchiefed girl had sold from her cart that morning. All their fathers had been eaten up by the war. Then, afterwards, came the famines and epidemics and deportations. His mother had had a cow that she loved whose name was Joyous. She sang to the cow and told her stories. Then she died of typhoid and the cow went into mourning and wouldn't give any milk and slowly turned into a bull. His grandmother said such things happened.

Later again, all the light drained from the dome of the sky and lay in an amber glow around its rim. The leaves turned black and the roofs of the houses turned black and everything sank down into the earth. The stars came out, myriads of stars all over a sky as vast as the land which was vast as an ocean. The sky made everything small — the dwellings, the forests around us, our lives. I sat on the steps and looked at the night. The man sat at the table and sang slow sad songs that came out of the 'Stans*, beating time with his open hand. The Milky Way was a deep wide road. The white-haired woman told me they called it the Road of the Slaves.

When we were home again I said this to Moya. It was because of that poem she'd written about the Milky Way —

*'Stans — countries of the former Soviet Bloc whose names end with '-stan', Kazakhstan, Uzbekistan, Turkmenistan etc.

Bealach na Bó Finne in Irish, the Path of the White Cow.

'. . . so many,' she quoted, her eyes gone inward, attentive, 'I had not thought death had undone so many . . .'

It was startling. You could hear the tramp of Empires. Millions undone on the Eastern edge of Europe.

Moldova, September 2003

Catalan Politics

We sat at the table,
bellies filled, laughing,
then something turned,
the two men began speaking,
softly and carefully,
all the time holding
each other's gaze.

The woman
changed the curve of her mouth,
stared down at the table,
made lines with her fork,
listened and drew;
anger, forbearance
tautened her eyes.

She spoke and emotion
throbbed in her voice.
The men heard her out,
then her husband was speaking,
quiet and rational,
his hand on the napkin,
folding it, knotting it,
tightening the knot
as he talked, as I watched thinking,
So. It's like this —
Just demands. Rights.
Quiet and rational.
Leave passion to women.
Yet this is the place
where civil wars start.

Guerra Civil

for Cesca Gelabert

The story begins to gather itself
before ever I see the picture.
Snippets of information
drift over our heads as we talk.

They begin to descend like the flakes
of pale ash that float in the air
after someone has placed a bomb
in a government office.

They lie on the table, then move
into clusters, like scraps of a jigsaw —
a gingery cat, a blue-and-white ball —
that a hand has begun to assemble.

It is then that she rises,
she climbs the steep stairs,
comes slowly back down,
the photograph clasped to her sweater.

She turns it around,
wipes off its dustless glass with her sleeve,
places before me a black-and-white print
of a couple walking a street.

They are both young. The man
has his head thrown far back, the woman,
all joy, holds tight to his arm
as she drags him towards the camera.

'My father,' she says.
'The woman's his sister,

she thought he was dead.
Yet here he is, back from the grave.'

Her father's story? *Servei Militar.*
Then *Guerra Civil.* After the *guerra*,
hard labour for years in North African camps.
This was the photo of when he came home.

She shrugs. Her lids drop. The scraps of grey ash
are falling and falling, the man on the table
has ancient eyes which are still seeing things
he doesn't want to be seeing.

On Not Visiting My Aunt in Hospital

You'd said, 'I don't want you to go,'
and the strange thing was that I didn't mind
though I ached all over and, outside the window,
the afternoon floated, golden with dust motes;
didn't mind sitting on, talking of this and of that,
answering questions I'd answered ten minutes before.
And afterwards, driving the long drive home,
I'd meant to go back the next day.

But along came the world, rattling and banging my door.
It made such a noise that I turned back the key in the lock.
In barged my life,
hands full of e-mails and faxes and phone-calls,
of things to be said, of tasks to be done,
and, fool that I was, I believed in the force of the world.

꙳

Now I'm out of bed once again. I could drive,
but instead I'm here
in the poplars' rustling shade.
The mountains are blue,
the wind's in the trees, the bees
are bumping about in the bells of the flowers.
And I don't want to leave this, I don't want to go there
and wilt in a hospital ward.
Forgive me. A few more days. I just can't make myself
stop the not-wanting of it.
And please do again what you did for me
when you told your friend that I came every day,
and then smiled at me with such sweetness
because you thought it was true.

After Rage

It was only
when I had carried the seedlings
out into the cold day,
when I had sat myself down
in the damp grass
and pricked out
hollyhocks, poppies, lavender, pinks —
the young plants,
the fibrous trail of their webby roots —
firming them
into their new places;
only then
did I quiet enough

for the great winds to die down
in the whitethorns of my being,
for the magpies to leave off their rattling
in the grace of the silver birch.

The Renunciation

for Seán

That was the day
that he made Death go from him,
though she was beautiful,
crowned with white bones,

her robe stuck with seed-pearls,
dried petals of lilies,
her face austere, tender,
half eaten-away.

'No,' he said, 'No,'
but she pressed close behind him,
turned as he turned,
breathed through his breath.

Then he wrapped both his hands
in the gauze of her sorrow,
stretched wide his arms
till the web pulled and tore.

OF THE MIDDLE

The High Pyrenees

I lifted my eyes and there was the sea of the mountains,
wave upon wave, and far out on the ocean, white peaks,

then the silence came close and stood there beside me and
    waited,
and I knew there was nothing to want or to fear or to say —

there was only the ancient sea of the mountains,
only the night coming down on the great dark slide of its
    waves.

The Dregs of the Year

for Colette Bryce

Small birds at the nuts in a frenzy of feeding;
winter
squeezing them
down to the bone.

Old sights, old sounds.
Ceremonial.
Winter,
her ancient ways.

And sheep,
            moving about the wet meadow.
And crows,
            adrift in the faded light.

Starlings.
The rush of their wings.
Bandit bands
whizzing above the drenched land.

Wind rocks the last shriveled hands
on the chestnut trees.
There's the wedge of a daylight moon
with a bleeding edge

and clouds
blowing over it.

Water. The world. Sodden.

The ash is a rag-tree of crows.

Ancestors

The young dog lies at my feet.
Wet still, she shivers and sleeps.
By the river, she was all hunter.

The river, filled with fresh rain,
was breaching itself, loosing sheets of new water
over its weirs and its banks.

The heron stood in the flood,
his old spirit strong and unruly.
Two swans drifted by, washed in beauty.
The straw of the rushes gleamed gold in the morning.

I threw in a stick, the old dog leapt first,
swam straight and fierce,
turned,
forged through black water, the stick in her mouth,
her eyes fixed always on mine.

She is stubborn and loyal and strong.
Sometimes she pits her will against mine
and I force her to bend,
and she bends but she will not submit.
She knows that I know, that I'm angry, admiring.

A picture hangs in this room, a detail from an Old Master.
Two women, at prayer,
swansdown for skin,
robes pearled and furred,
missals at rest in their hands.
A long way behind them the black-coated painter,
bony in flesh and in spirit,
stares from the depths of his picture.

He breaches his painting, pours himself through
the gap of his eyes

and right into mine
pours the fresh shock of new water.

The young dog yelps in her sleep and gives chase.
The old dog lies on her side, her eyes wide.
Always these old ones, on watch down the years.

Mrs George Departs

i.m. my aunt, Eve George

First there were two of us,
then there was one.

All night,
and I never lifted my eyes off you.

So how did you pull off
this conjuring trick?

How did you slip past —
so fleet on your feet —

that I only knew you were gone
when I heard the click of the closing door?

Late May

The dew falling
and the night falling
and the lambs crying,

and the trees standing
proud and tender
in the still, cold air.

February Snow

The fields are mud.
The first buds on the ash trees
blacken to spear points: stubby, stubbornly raised.

The mountains, ink-blue on their lower slopes,
stand in white silence on a sky
grown passionate with snow-cloud.

Strange visitors,
come to us out of marvellous lands,
proud with a great still pride.

In Catalonia

Above the snowline
I entered the place of the silence;
walked into a room,
the door swinging closed behind.

Only a scatter of snow — the winter, beginning —
but darkness was near,
and the cattle and sheep
and birds had moved down.

Then I knew the shape of the silence,
its old, fierce indifference.
A presence come out of the halls of the mountain,
wearing no flesh.

Jacob and the Angel, Wrestling

for Graeme Williamson

This morning I read about Jacob wrestling the angel.
And of his dream.
About the ladder reaching to heaven,
threaded with angels *ascending, descending*.

This life, here on earth. Who has not wrestled an angel?
All night *till the breaking of day*.
Blind. Pressed close as lovers.
Consumed in the fetid sweat of the flesh,
the terrible reek of power from an angel.
Thy name shall no more be called Jacob, but Israel.

Rising up, weak and spent in the morning,
a strange name branded onto the brow,
a nameless horror still clinging.

OF LOVE AND LONGING

A Peacock at La Cartuja

A half-restored Cathusian monastery, northeast of Seville

Oh lonely, lonely, the heat,
the sun in the glittering sky,
the peacock's blank cry on the light,
the rattle of God in his thighs.

Enclosed in the netted vines,
his great fan erect on the air,
he turns himself, silent and slow,
around and around and around.

At dusk on the side of the hill
the peahen starts up her creaking.
In the din of the day she is mute.
With darkness, this rackety calling.

The church and the humming grass.
At dawn, in the stifling noon.
And the sun, the sun, the beat of the sun,
and the ancient light of the evening.

Your China-poem Came in the Post

for Sinéad Morrissey

When I'd finished reading
your poem about your time in China
I wanted to go upstairs
and unpack from some old chest
a length
of saffron-yellow silk.

Silk,
not slithery but stiff,
encrusted with the stuff of being nothing
but itself.
And the enfolding air,
cast off now, but infused, fusty,
with its preciousness
and its yellow being.

I don't know why
this came upon me,
it was something to do
with the unrolled bolt of your journey
and that last part when China
met China in the market place
and they conversed.

You know, the world, when it's smalled down
to what can be seen through two eyes,
is too big and too full of fear,
it cannot be grasped,
it can only be turned into yellow silk
and watched from a kneeling place on the floor,
then
after a long time

touched
        so the touch
yields up a lost domain.

In Berne

I want to be, however briefly,
a woman, fleshy, twenty-eight or nine,
with thick hair, braided, its escaping tendrils
curling and warm, sweat-pasted at the neck.
I want to have dense skin, an arse that sways,
to feel my breasts rest heavy in my hands,
to scent with musk the swish of gathered skirts.
I want to know how food would taste to such a woman,
to live the life her flesh would open for me,
to lift a dark-green bottle to my mouth,
then lean from that lit window near the roof
and call down as he passes, far below.

Travelling

We spoke of the girl who'd appeared before dinner one night in the kitchen, then disappeared. Like the girl in the fairy tale who dresses in animal skins and lives under the stairs, but slips out when the moment is right and puts on her dress of stars to make soup for the prince. I didn't say this to him, I said only that she was beautiful. He said that, talking to her, he had felt his legs go weak. Who was she? I asked. He told me she was a teacher, he thought she might have come from the village but now she lived somewhere else. I said she looked too young and he said yes. I said I didn't think she knew how beautiful she was. He said yes again and then we fell silent or maybe we talked about something else.

I can see her now in my mind's eye, her eyes, the curve of her sweater, her bee-stung lips. These glimpses. I am glad I am old enough and passionate enough to love the way she was, to love her for being in the world, sometimes clothed in animal skins, sometimes wearing a dress of stars. Age can bring envy of youth but these days it mostly brings sweetness. The more I love, the more I love. I knew she had placed a ring in the bowl of soup that he'd drunk from her hand without even knowing he was drinking as they talked. He was a Youngest Son with a silver tongue, he was searching, but it had been a long time, and he might give up on the quest. He had lost his silver tongue when he talked to her, but the silver had flowed down into his veins — I saw it as I watched him drinking the soup, I saw how it shone.

After she'd gone he looked down into the bowl and there was the ring of gold.

If he looks for a girl in a dress of stars he will never find her. If he takes his hounds and hunts in the woods they will circle the bole of a hollow tree and bay at the girl who crouches inside, dirty and thin in her animal hides. Then, to call off his hounds and throw her the dress made of moonlight.

But there is a woman at home who waits. What can we do

when life opens itself and allows us these glimpses? Is it fidelity that is asked of us, or fortitude? It's a hard one, that. We cannot undo what we've done nor unsee what we've seen. When we go home we must sit by the fire and talk and eat meat and forget the strange skies we've lain beneath and the strange, bright stars that burn there. It is forbidden to speak of these things. And, besides, there is no one at home who can hear.

Treading Air

for Wu Xinwei

The door — open on to the morning.
The mauve call of a pigeon
in the heavy darkness of the chestnut tree.

So many miles to have travelled away.
Now — at last — again —
the garden and the morning.

The light — flittery, broken. The shine
of light on wind-turned leaves.
To be not here.
To be here again.
Home
to the morning.
Pigeons,
their blue-grey, wide-winged glide
                              down to the grass.

Being away: the furthest point
is when the heart turns, makes for home
while travelling on.
After that, it's all with the people.
Faces
bright — sad — breaking open.

Being home.
Being there with them still, while being home.

The jackdaws, squabbling on the roof-tiles.
And starting again
                    with the garden.

Communication

for my mother

My father wouldn't talk on the phone.
He gave it to my mother,
then told her what to say to me.
He seemed to need this go-between.
As though without, I was too raw —
the whole complicated business
too risky, too much effort.
My brother is the same,
he phones someone and, if they're in,
he hangs up, rings back later for the answer-phone.

I am less sure —
I think I have to do these things, to prise myself loose
from my nature. Sometimes, after a long call,
I feel betrayed into words
I have not thought through, accused
because I do not want this miracle.
I am too slow to move so fast.

Alone in the house, I let the phone ring for days.
I don't turn on stereo or radio or television.
The membrane of the walls thins like muslin, the light
presses through. Wind sounds, bird sounds,
field sounds of cattle and sheep.
The swish of the crows flowing over.
I live deep in the world
and I grow like my father.

Awake

This morning I woke with a flame in my heart.
Grand statement. Yet joyous, playful. Meaning
an open heart at the open window,
air thin and high,
the builders' radio, vapid with music,
the chink of their tools against rock.
Flowers in a jar — stone parsley, vetch,
stalks of late hyssop, violet with blooms.
More hammers and chisels, a moving of timber,
one of them lights up, coughs himself clear.
A magpie sits high on the ridge of the roof
that slices across the ridge of the mountain.

Sometimes these days don't come, or stay hidden,
sometimes it rains so long you forget the sun.
Or the other way round. Now the magpie starts up —
rogue bird of gossip and plague and complaint —
he cackles and bounces his rage, his delight,
at credulous simpletons searching for goodness.

Hit the Ground, Running

Hurry up, hurry up,
already it's leaving,

and life rushes off
through the hips of that girl
in the front of the queue,
through the eyes of the young man
who's watching and longing,
life rushes on, both arms
flung open —

Joy

The gulls on the sand
when the tide has pulled clear
in the morning.

Three of them stand
in the shine of the strand,
the sky out to sea blowing clean.

Suzanna

for Pat Murphy

It was one of those hard funerals. A man, not old, not young, dead not through disease or an outside agent. And full summer, the great trees burgeoning, the brothers waiting, quiet at the door.

I walked in, sat down, glanced over. She was there in the pew on the other side of the aisle. I barely knew her, didn't dislike her. Perhaps I thought her *a bit much*.

The funeral mass, its pattern of word and gesture. We rose from our seats. The shouldered coffin, the cleave of its prow through the wash of green light at the door. It was harder for her, he'd been in and out of her childhood; I hadn't known him, had come on account of the feeling I had for one of the brothers. When we met in the aisle she reached and took hold of my hand and she didn't let go.

Rain came. The priest sped the rosary, wind streamed the trees.

Later, at the long tables, she chose the seat next to mine. Funeral meats, bread without hunger. Talk with the brothers, the wives, the nephews and nieces.

From that day I felt her hand always in mine, and I loved her.

October

All the hillside is blazing
in the hot gold light,
every dying leaf,
blazing —

And the dew-soaked pasture.
And the high sky, sailing with cloud-kites.

And over the ridge, the cirrus wisps
in shining threads of fine, spun hair.

∾

Forgetfulness
up here in the mountains —
my old, slow river, its loved remembrance,
fades like a photograph emptied out by the sun.

In Bed Again

after reading Tu Fu

Five-thirty. February dusk.
The last few tits and finches,
black in the netted branches of the silver birch,
flitter and loop the hanging feeders.
The wheelbarrow lies on its side in the long wet grass,
its yellow handles
rusting into gloom. How tired I am.
But quiet too. Better this
than the exhausted rage that sickness lays
upon my doorstep, as a cat his kill.
How still the garden;
still the rowan and ash. The first lambs
stagger the muddy field. Life passes
slowly, slowly. And all the while
the furious horses gallop
over the endless reaches of the yellow plain.

THE WAY THINGS ARE

Solitude

It was January.
I'd hardly seen anyone for days.
The sheep were all sitting separate and silent,
a hard wind was coming in over the hill,
a white moon floated.

I'd bought the pumpkin for soup.
My arms had dropped with the weight of it,
dropped and come back, like the bounce back up into air
after the deep of the river.
I'd hefted it in from the car,
set it down on the table.
It was smaller and fiercer and redder than I'd expected.

I was out on the hill for the sake of the moon
and the ash trees, raking the way with shadow.
Where the road ran high the fields slid into the valley;
cloud covered the slopes of the mountains
laying down snow.
I carried the colour, red fire on the dark of the table,
the colour would bear me through till his return.

When I got home the phone was ringing,
I had the key in the door but it wouldn't turn.
I heard the phone cease in the empty house.
And the dogs milled about.
And the pumpkin stared out at the moon.

Gale Forecast

A hard wind
raids from the sea.

My mother's a storm gull,
blown over the strand,

her bones are gone hollow
and light and ready for flight.

Monasterio de la Cartuja

There was a pool, yes.
Dinner on the terrace.
Even a sign that read 'Recepción'.

After a week we began to arrive.
Circling and feinting,
we edged our way inwards.

Sparrows threaded the walnut tree.
Shadows of finches
fluttered the ochre wall.

A cock's voice printed the cloudy mornings.
The cat rushed,
her eyes wild.

The great church stood in the humming grass —
at dawn, in the heat of the afternoon,
at gnat-shine in the evening light.

All that was there was there always:
a spring well that never ran dry
bubbling on to the plateau.

Sunrise peoples,
their drub-throb trawling the sea of the darkness,
snagging the Orb of Light.

Then Romans, Moors, Carthusians.
The circle,
always complete and without accumulation.

Winter

It is dusk, the stone mountains stretch
across the smeared blood
of the eaten sun.

A coughing behind.
The cattle are moving
from high ground to low.

Dun cows on dun grass.
Their neat forms dissolve,
resolve into night.

Derrynane '05

It was well after seven,
but how could we leave?
It would have been
like spitting in the face of God.
A cormorant surfaced and dived,
surfaced and dived, blue shadows
lay down in the scuffled footprints,
the long, glass waves curled over
and broke into spatters of light.

Yellow rattle, eyebright, bedstraw,
sea holly, milkwort.
Nobody there but us.
We stayed on — the pale sand, the evening,
the islands all turning
smoke-blue and floating away —
stayed as we'd done so often before,
but might not again,
the times being frailer,
everything being frailer.
Old ways fall away,
the cormorant's wings beat
black on the water,
the world's going spinning off
to God-knows-where.

Up There

for Robert Adamson

The bright-coloured plastic pegs on the line catch the bright autumn sun. In the night some spider has travelled the pegs which are joined now by fine silken threads like the links in joined-up writing. They shine in the light. *Birds of the Blue Mountains* tells of warblers that weave hanging nests out of bark and grass, then encircle them with scavenged cobwebs.

Once I saw a whole balaclava made out of cobwebs, spun into yarn, then knitted. It was greyish and asked to be touched but they'd put it into a case of glass to protect it from reaching hands. (There were other fingerprints on the glass so I knew it wasn't just me.) Some artists have strange, un-useful imaginations that feed on the impossible and draw it close. This may be unwise. If Arachne had stuck to modest household weavings she'd never have got above herself and challenged the Goddess, ending up as a dangling spinner of webs and threads.

Threads. It's all about paying attention and following where they lead. Somewhere behind the house there's a rabble of birds in a eucalyptus, they chatter and squabble and talk. There are sudden explosive squawks from the neighbouring trees, a whistle drops from the heights. Now a quarrelsome murmuring slowly, slowly subsides. I don't know these calls, nor what the birds look like that own these enormous voices. I go out to search, but the trees here run up and up into the sky, their leaves all muddled with light that confuses my eyes. Such big splashes of sound swoop out of the branches. They plunge down, catch my attention, then fly it up high and weave it into their high green kingdom.

Pied Currawongs

Currawongs like to be plural, to cruise in a gang,
wearing heavy black beaks
and round yellow eyes made of glass.
Busy and wicked, they drop from the trees
to sit on the fence round the compost heap,
bounce down to scavenge the leavings,
then rise up in monstrous alarm when I open the door.

This is all sham. They are unafraid.
At light-fade they sit in the branches,
whistling and squabbling
like knives in a drawer
that someone's shut tight for the night.

A currawong resembles an oversized magpie crossed with a crow, but minus the magpie's black rattle, and minus his boat-tail to balance and glide.

Blue Mountains

for Jacki Parry

Out there is all sunlight and shadow.
The compost heap heaves with currawongs.
Something bright squawks in the trees.

This vast, hard country.
This light that glitters and opens distance.

Fathers

When she met him, months later, in the shopping centre, he told her his father had died. They sat down together to talk. He said his parents had split long before, that his father's heart had been failing for years. He said he had thought him a hard, sour man, but in that last month he had gone there and a sort of tenderness had flowed. Now he walked dazed in the world.

She said her father was old but fit, had died just like that — no warning sickness. One minute there, filling up life; the next, and an emptiness like electricity occupied his space.

He said he'd met a woman in the spring whose father-in-law was dying slowly of liver failure. The father-in-law told her husband, his son, that he wished he had never been born. And he didn't mean himself. Then he'd died in the night, the words unretracted.

They sat in the rainy summer light under the high glass roof of the shopping centre. He said there were two sorts of people in the world. Those whose fathers had died, and those whose hadn't.

The waiter came and they argued briefly over which of them would pay for one coffee, one tea. Then they got up from their seats and stumbled out into the city.

Journey

for Brendan Looby

Petunias with magenta faces
glow through the scrubby all-year shrubs
beneath the station wall.

How are ye keepin', Kevin?

The train is late, the morning cloudy.
A few crows dander on the warm grey air,
a heron glides its slow grey glide above the trees.

The train pulls in, we all climb on.

The fields stand in the stillness.
Dust-gold with harvest. Textured. Heavy.
The sun burns off the shoals that swim the sky.

We flicker through

each field and pasture flown before the eye can settle
and, stopping in Athy beside the graveyard,
the life in us so rank and undefeated,

we somehow think the dead are not related.

We flicker through our lives, our phones engaged,
speed on the straights, lean into curves, slow for the stations —
sometimes to glimpse at dusk, or when rain veils the windows,

eyes startled, fearful, floating in the glass.

Behold

Look at the last of the cherries,
their burned red flare
against the smoke-walls of the mountains.

Cack, cack. The raven, high overhead,
big wings catching the light.

Look at the ash,
its lemon-gold fronds
against the blue blaze of the sky.

Butterflies, tiny, yellower than yolk,
drinking the dandelions.

Look at the poplars,
their flesh growing luminous,
limbs pushing through like black bones.

A little wind stirs in the quiet,
blowing the shadows about.

Look at the death of the year,
its silence, its beauty,
lying across the lit meadows.

Acknowledgements

Acknowledgements are due to the editors of the following publications where some of these poems, or versions of them, were published first: James Joyce Bloomsday Magazine 2004, *Metre, Missouri Review, New Hibernia Review/Iris Éireannach Nua,* Oxfam Calendar 2005, *Parabola, Ploughshares* and *The Stinging Fly.*

The author wishes to thank the Centre d'Art i Natura, Farrera, Catalonia, Spain; The Patrick and Katherine Kavanagh Fellowship; The James Joyce Foundation for the Suspended Sentence Award; the Varuna Writers' Centre, Australia, for time spent there; the Chinese Writers' Association, who hosted the visit to Beijing; and Hawthornden International Writers' Retreat, Scotland.